Northwest Territories

Journey Across Canada

Harry Beckett

The Rourke Book Co., Inc.
Vero Beach, Florida 32964

Harry Beckett M.A. (Cambridge), M.Ed. (Toronto), Dip.Ed. (Hull,
England) has taught at the elementary and high school levels in
England, Canada, France, and Germany. He has also travelled widely
for a tour operator and a major book company.

Edited by Laura Edlund
Laura Edlund received her B.A. in English literature from the University
of Toronto and studied Writing for Multimedia and Book Editing and
Design at Centennial College. She has been an editor since 1986 and a
traveller always.

ACKNOWLEDGMENTS
For photographs: Geovisuals (Kitchener, Ontario), The Canadian
Tourism Commission and its photographers.
For reference: *The Canadian Encyclopedia, Encarta 1997, The Canadian
Global Almanac, Symbols of Canada. Canadian Heritage*, Reproduced
with the permission of the Minister of Public Works and Government
Services Canada, 1997.
For maps: Promo-Grafx of Collingwood, Ont., Canada.

Library of Congress Cataloging-in-Publication Data

Beckett, Harry, 1936-
   Northwest Territories / Harry Beckett.
     p. cm. — (Journey across Canada)
   Includes index.
   Summary: Examines the size, location, weather, industries, and
festivals of the Northwest Territories, which make up one third of the
Canadian land mass.
   ISBN 1-55916-207-4
   1. Northwest Territories—Juvenile literature. [1.Northwest Territories.]
I. Title II. Series: Beckett, Harry, 1936- Journey across Canada
F1060.35.B43 1997
971.9'2—dc21
                                                97-22219
                                                CIP
                                                  AC

Printed in the USA

TABLE OF CONTENTS

Size and Location 5

Geography: Land and Water 6

What Is the Weather Like? 8

Making a Living: Harvesting the Land 11

From the Earliest Peoples 12

Making a Living: From Industry 14

If You Go There 17

Major Cities 18

Signs and Symbols 20

Glossary 23

Index 24

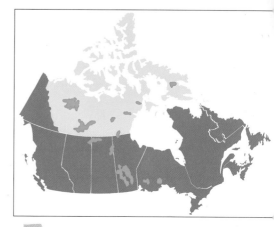

Nunavut
Boundary

Ellesmere
Island

*ARCTIC
OCEAN*

ARCTIC

*Beaufort
Sea*

Resolute

A R C H I P E L A G O

B a f f i n   I s l a n d

*Great
Bear Lake*

Arctic Circle

Iqaluit

Norman
Wells

Mackenzie Mountains

Mackenzie River

MACKENZIE
VALLEY
AREA

ARCTIC

MAINLAND

Yellowknife

*Nahanni
River*

*Great
Slave Lake*

Hay River

HUDSON BAY
LOWLAND

*H u d s o n
B a y*

N

W   E

S

**NORTHWEST
TERRITORIES**

*James
Bay*

Chapter One

SIZE AND LOCATION

The Northwest Territories, or N.W.T., include the northernmost areas of Canada. Land that was once part of N.W.T. now makes up Alberta, Saskatchewan, Manitoba, and the Yukon, plus parts of Ontario and Québec. On April 1, 1999 the Northwest Territories will change again—the eastern portion will become a new territory called Nunavut.

The territories are huge—equalling over 3 million square kilometres (over 2 million square miles), or about one third the total size of Canada.

From the Yukon, the territories extend east to Baffin Island, north of Québec and Newfoundland. From the borders with Manitoba, Saskatchewan, Alberta, and B.C., they reach Canada's northern limits. The islands in Hudson Bay and James Bay are also part of the territories.

Find out more...

- The territories extend to just 720 kilometres (447 miles) south of the North Pole.
- Nunavut's total land area will be 2 121 102 square kilometres (819 022 square miles).
- Nunavut means "our land" in the Inuit language, Inuktitut.

Chapter Two

GEOGRAPHY: LAND AND WATER

Three geographic regions make up most of N.W.T.—the Arctic Archipelago, the eastern Arctic Mainland, and the western Mackenzie Valley area. The first two regions are beyond the **tree line** (TREE line) and will roughly form Nunavut.

The Arctic **Archipelago** (ar kuh PEL uh goe) includes all the territories' islands. The northeastern islands are mountainous and ice-capped, but the southern islands are flat, rocky **tundra** (TUN druh).

Ellesmere Island. Icebergs often float in the channels between the rocky northern islands.

The wide delta of the Mackenzie River—Canada's longest river, at 4241 kilometres (2365 miles).

The Arctic Mainland lies on the **Canadian Shield** (kuh NAY dee un SHEELD). It is rolling tundra, with many scattered lakes and long rivers. The region is also known as the Barren Lands.

To the west, is the Mackenzie Valley area. It includes the Mackenzie River valley and the Mackenzie Mountains. Except in the far north, it is forested. In the valley, the **permafrost** (PUR muh frost) thaws to form large swamps each summer.

7

Chapter Three

WHAT IS THE WEATHER LIKE?

Half of the territories' land lies north of the **Arctic Circle** (ARK tik SUR kul). The winters are very long, very cold, and generally dry. However, the climate does vary.

The far north of the Arctic Archipelago is the coldest region. Even in summer, icebergs float off the island shores. The icy waters keep the summers cool, about 4°C (39.2° F), but also bring fog and cloud cover. The Arctic Mainland is less affected by the ocean, and its summers are a few degrees warmer.

The Mackenzie Valley and the eastern islands close to the North Atlantic Ocean are the least cold. Here there is more snow and rain. Summers in the Mackenzie Valley area last three warm months and are quite like those in the provinces to the south.

Find out more...

- Yellowknife has average temperatures of -28.8°C (-19.8° F) in January and 16.3°C (61.3° F) in July.
- Resolute has average temperatures of -32.1°C (-25.8° F) in January and 4.1°C (39.4° F) in July.

During the short summer, the tundra comes alive with small blossoms.

Chapter Four

MAKING A LIVING: HARVESTING THE LAND

Agriculture is only a very small part of life in the territories. Poor soil, few frost-free days, and permafrost make it easier to buy food from elsewhere. Some fresh vegetables are grown in the south and southwest.

Hunting, trapping, and fishing are important in daily life. Many people earn some part of their living from wildlife, especially in smaller communities. Caribou herds in the Arctic Mainland are a key source of food. The traditional fur trade is becoming less important because of lower demand. Near Great Slave Lake, some fish are caught to sell.

Small sawmills in the Mackenzie Valley provide lumber and wood for fuel. However, the trees are small and slow-growing, and the forests are remote.

The Inuit of the Arctic coast and islands hunt sea mammals for meat and skins.

Find out more...

- Moose, polar bear, beaver, fox, muskrat, and migratory birds are also hunted or trapped.
- About 615 000 square kilometres (237 370 square miles) of the territories are forested.

11

Chapter Five

FROM THE EARLIEST PEOPLES

The earliest peoples in the territories may have come across a land bridge from Asia.

Traditionally, the **Inuit** (IN yoo it) hunted and fished on the Arctic shores, or hunted inland for caribou. They lived in snowhouses—or igloos—in winter and homes made of sod, stone, animal skins, or whalebone in summer.

In the Mackenzie Valley area, the **Dene** (DE nay) gathered plants and hunted. They used snowshoes,

Inuit man, dressed in furs, in front of an animal skin teepee

Part of the Northwest Territories team at the Arctic Winter Games

sleds, and toboggans for winter travel, and canoes in summer.

Eventually Vikings, European explorers, whalers, fur traders, missionaries, and miners came. Many explorers, including Franklin, came looking for the Northwest Passage to the Pacific.

More than half the population is Inuit, Dene, or **Métis** (MAY tee), who make their living in both traditional and non-traditional ways. Most non-Native people live in the Mackenzie Valley area.

13

Chapter Six

MAKING A LIVING: FROM INDUSTRY

Mining produces much of the wealth of the Northwest Territories. There are deposits of zinc, lead, gold, and other valuable metals. Only the gold is processed in the area.

Oil has been produced at Norman Wells since 1921. The oil exploration industry has made other large finds, but many have not yet been developed fully. They are remote, or there are concerns about the environment and Native land claims.

In transportation, the vast distances and limited roads make air travel the lifeline of most settlements. Highways are mostly all-weather gravel, and winter roads may be tracks over frozen lakes. The Mackenzie River is a transportation corridor from the interior to the coast.

Find out more...

- Large reserves of oil have been found in the Beaufort Sea, and of natural gas in the southwest.
- Tourism and diamond mining are both developing industries.

One in six Native people is involved in the important arts and craft industry.

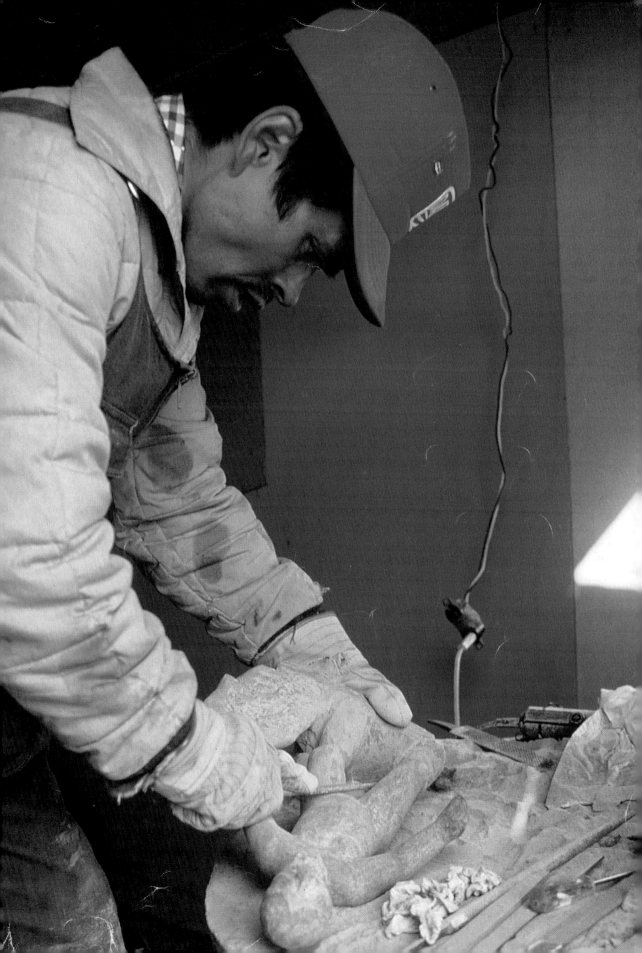

Chapter Seven

IF YOU GO THERE...

The magnificent scenery and a wide variety of wildlife in Auyuittuq, Wood Buffalo, and Nahanni National Parks attract many visitors from the south. Nahanni, a United Nations World Heritage site, has hot springs and a waterfall almost one and a half times the height of Niagara.

Visitors also watch for the **aurora borealis** (o ROR uh bor ee Al is) and for inukshuks. These Inuit stone figures were used to mark trails for travellers.

Annually the Sunrise Festival celebrates the first day of sunlight after a month of darkness. Every two years, northern athletes compete in traditional Native and other sports at the Arctic Winter Games.

Inukshuks are sometimes used to drive caribou into the water, so that they are easier to hunt.

Find out more...

- Yellowknife holds a Caribou Carnival and the Midnight Classic Golf Tournament.
- Hay River holds an Ookpik Carnival, named for the Inuit handicraft of an Arctic owl.

Chapter Eight

MAJOR CITIES

Yellowknife, the capital of the Northwest Territories, began as a fur trading centre. It was named for a Native people of the area. Gold rushes brought people in the 1930s and 1940s. Good roads, air travel, and new hydro-electric power plants have made the city even more attractive.

Yellowknife lies on the northern arm of Great Slave Lake, in an area of rocky outcrops and stunted vegetation.

Iqaluit means "place where the fish are."

Yellowknife is a busy city of government, mining, transportation, communication, and tourism, but still a small friendly northern town.

Iqaluit is Baffin region's transportation, communication, and education centre. It stands on the site of a traditional fishing camp, at the head of Frobisher Bay on Baffin Island. Iqaluit is a centre for fishing, sealing, carving, handicrafts, and tourism and was chosen to be Nunavut's capital.

Chapter Nine

SIGNS AND SYMBOLS

The flag shows three panels—two narrow blue panels on either side of a white panel with the territorial shield on it. Blue and white represent the lakes, waters, ice, and snow of the territories.

The territorial shield has a white upper segment, split by a wavy blue line, representing the polar ice pack and the Northwest Passage. Below, a green area (symbolizing the forested areas) and a red area (symbolizing the Barren Lands) are separated by a diagonal line (representing the tree line). The gold bars and the white fox mask refer to minerals and furs, which are important to the North.

The shield is repeated in the coat of arms. Two narwhal whales guard a compass rose, symbolic of the North Pole.

The territories' flower is the mountain avens, a member of the rose family.

Northwest Territories' flag, coat of arms, and flower

GLOSSARY

archipelago (ar kuh PEL uh goe) — island group

Arctic Circle (ARK tik SUR kul) — a parallel (66° 32') north of the equator above which the sun does not set during midsummer and does not rise during midwinter

aurora borealis (o ROR uh bor ee AL is) — shows of coloured lights in northern skies

Canadian Shield (kuh NAY dee un SHEELD) — a horseshoe-shaped area of rock in Canada

Dene (DE nay) — an Athapaskan Native people

Inuit (IN yoo it) — a Native people living mainly in northern Canada, etc.; also known as Eskimos

Métis (MAY tee) — French, meaning person of mixed ancestry, especially French and Native

permafrost (PUR muh frost) — ground that is always frozen at, or just below, the surface

tree line (TREE line) — a point beyond which trees will not grow because of the climate

tundra (TUN dra) — treeless, arctic, permafrost plain

The aurora borealis or Northern Lights

INDEX

Arctic Archipelago   6, 8,
Arctic Circle   8
Arctic Mainland   6, 7, 8,
   11, 20
climate   8, 11, 14, 17
explorers and settlers
   13
fishing, hunting, fur trade
   11, 12, 13, 18, 19, 20
forests   6, 7, 11, 20
Iqaluit   19
lakes and rivers   7, 11,
   14, 17, 18, 20
Mackenzie Valley area
   6, 7, 8, 11, 12, 13, 14

mining   13, 14, 18,
   19, 20
Native peoples   5, 11,
   12, 13, 14, 17, 18
Nunavut   5, 6, 19
tourism   14, 17, 19
transportation   12, 13
   14, 18, 19
wildlife   8, 11, 12,
   17, 20
Yellowknife   8, 17,
   18, 19